The Library of
NATIVE AMERICANS™

The Mono
of California

Jack S. Williams

The Rosen Publishing Group's
PowerKids Press™
New York

For my friend David Martínez, who never forgot the meaning of standing by his ancestors

Published in 2004 by The Rosen Publishing Group, Inc.
29 East 21st Street, New York, NY 10010

Photo and illustration credits: cover, p. 27 courtesy of the Division of Anthropology Archives Office, American Museum of Natural History, Catalog # .50.1/2127, Catalog # 50/2708; p. 4 © Lee White/Corbis; p. 7 courtesy of the C. Hart Merriam Collection of Native American Photographs, The Bancroft Library, University of California, Berkeley; p. 8 courtesy of the Phoebe Apperson Hearst Museum of Anthropology and the Regents of the University of California, photographed by Edward W. Gifford, Unit ID: 15-7023, Unit ID 15-7025; pp. 9, 10 © Joe McDonald/Corbis; pp. 12, 28, 30, 49 National Anthropological Archives, Smithsonian Institution, INV #00859400, INV #01576600, INV #00859300, SPC Basin Paiute BAE 4720 00860800; p. 16 © Joseph Sohm/Photo Researchers, Inc.; p. 17 © D. Robert & Lorri Franz/Corbis; pp. 19, 24 courtesy of the Phoebe Apperson Hearst Museum of Anthropology and the Regents of the University of California, Photographed by Nellie T. MacGraw Hedgpeth, Unit ID: 15-209544, Unit ID 15-20942; p. 20 © Phil Schermeister/Corbis; pp. 22, 42, 44 Library of Congress Prints and Photographs Division; pp. 34, 54 National Archives and Records Administration; p. 36 © Galen Rowell/Corbis; p. 38 68-56-1-2: *Father Serra Celebrates Mass at Monterey*, Leon Trousset, oil on canvas, 1876, California Historical Society Fine Arts Collection; p. 45 © Hulton Archive/ Getty Images; p. 47 Ft. Tejon Historical Association; p. 50 © Pauline Horton, Papilio/Corbis; p. 52 AP Photo/ Damian Dovarganes, File; p. 56 courtesy of Dr. Chick Herbert.

Book Design: Geri Fletcher; Editor: Charles Hofer; Photo Researcher: Sherri Liberman

Williams, Jack S.
The Mono of California / Jack S. Williams. — 1st ed.
    p. cm. — (The library of Native Americans)
Summary: Describes the origins, history, and culture of the Mono people from what is now California, from prehistory to the present.
Includes bibliographical references and index.
ISBN 1-4042-2662-1 (lib. bdg.)
1. Mono Indians—History—Juvenile literature. 2. Mono Indians—Social life and customs—Juvenile literature. [1. Mono Indians. 2. Indians of North America—California.] I. Title. II. Series.
E99.M86W55 2004
979.4004'97457—dc22
                                                                                          2003015592

Manufactured in the United States of America

On the cover: A Mono basket.

A variety of terminologies has been employed in works about Native Americans. There are sometimes differences between the original names or terms used by a Native American group and the anglicized or modernized versions of such names or terms. Although this book contains terms that we feel will be most recognizable to our readership, there may also exist synonymous or native words that are preferred by certain speakers.

Contents

One

Introducing the Mono People

The high-desert mountains that guard the eastern border of California have a strange and even fantastic appearance. A traveler who climbs into these highlands passes through gentle, grass-covered slopes and valleys. Clouds can actually form on the surface of the land, even as the sun bathes the mountains in bright light. Even in June, cold temperatures can crystallize the water vapor in the air into microscopic snowflakes. If a person looks toward the sun, the surrounding world is filled with the reflections of tiny fragments of ice that look like sparkling dust. The pioneers called these strange atmospheric effects diamond dust.

The landscape of the region has other unexpected surprises. One of the strangest places is Mono Lake. Its grassy shores surround blue waters. In the center of the lake is an ancient volcanic cone, crusted with curious salt formations. If you did not know it was in California, you might guess that Mono Lake belonged on another planet.

The name of this unusual lake is shared by an important Native American nation. The Mono are a prominent California people. Most scholars divide them into eastern and western divisions. The

Mono Lake was an important part of the Mono world. Natural rock formations, made of the mineral travertine, dot the lake's shoreline. Today, Mono Lake is a popular destination for tourists.

The Mono Territory

Area of Detail

California

NEVADA
CALIFORNIA

Nisenan

Washo

Mono Lake
Northern
Paiute

Sierra Miwok

Owens Valley
Paiute-Shoshone

Monache

Western
Shoshone

Southern
Valley
Yokut

Foothill Yokut

Chumash

Tabtulabal

easterners include the Owens Valley Paiute-Shoshone and the Mono Lake Northern Paiute. The Western Mono are called the Monache.

No one is certain how many Mono people were living in California when the first European explorers arrived in North America, around 1492. Experts have suggested that there might have been between 3,000 and 5,000 Mono in the region.

The Mono Nation has always had to work hard to survive in the face of natural and man-made challenges. This has been especially true since the arrival of large numbers of outsiders, which began around 1850. Despite the

This map *(left)* illustrates the Mono territory along the California–Nevada border. The world of the Mono was dramatic and beautiful and included Mono Lake, pictured above in 1938.

7

8   The Mono people have a long and proud history. Their culture and way of life would be challenged in a changing world.

demands placed on them by many generations of invaders, these proud people have continued their struggle for justice and the survival of their beliefs and customs.

The Mono people moved to their homeland thousands of years ago. Some scholars have tried to determine where they came from. In that long-ago era, no one kept any written records. Archaelogists and linguistic anthropologists have worked together to create a general picture of how the Mono arrived in California. Archaeologists are researchers who study the remains left behind by earlier civilizations. Linguistic anthropologists study how languages are created and change over time.

Several pieces of evidence point to the fact that people came to North America sometime between 13,000 and 40,000 years ago. These travelers came from the eastern part of Asia using a narrow bridge made up of ice and tiny islands. These first Americans arrived searching for

The Mono region was dotted with mountain lakes. The Mono lived closely with the land, drawing from its endless resources.

9

food. They were probably following large herds of grazing animals, such as caribou. Each year, the hunters followed these creatures farther and farther south. Eventually, the newcomers had occupied all of North America and South America. The ancestors of the Mono were among these groups.

The Mono language is similar to the ones used by many other Native American nations. Experts call this common tongue Shoshone. The earliest version of this language probably developed over several hundred or even a thousand years. The Shoshone-speaking nations eventually occupied a very large part of North America that stretched

Following herds of animals such as caribou, the first inhabitants of North America entered the continent across a land bridge.

from California to Texas and north to Wyoming. By about 2000 BC, the ancestors of the western Shoshone nations settled into the Nevada region. Some of these people decided to move to the south and west. Their advances into new lands eventually brought them into eastern California. The Mono probably absorbed the people already living in the region. It is possible that they forced other nations out. No one can say for sure why the Mono ancestors decided to move. They may have been forced to move by droughts or other environmental disasters. It is also possible that the population grew so large that there was a need to discover new sources of food and water.

Some Native Americans say that the archaeologists and linguistic anthropologists are wrong. They argue that their ancestors had been created at the places where they were found by outsiders.

Two
Daily Life

Many modern visitors have a hard time imagining how Native Americans survived in the Mono territories. The land seems so rugged and empty. The first European visitors to the region thought that the Mono way of life was very strange. They called the clothes, jewelry, houses, tools, and religion of these people "primitive." Some people even imagined that the Mono hibernated like bears in caves. Almost none of the early visitors understood the truth. The Mono people had developed amazing methods to live in a land where there were few obvious resources. They had a lifestyle that was filled with natural and man-made beauty. The Mono were different from other peoples, but they were neither poorer nor inferior.

Living in a Land with Many Faces

The Mono's mountainous homeland in eastern California and western Nevada is made up of several geographic regions. The western border of the territory is the Sierra Nevada. This mountain chain includes the tallest place in the Mono's territory, Mount Whitney, which towers an incredible 14,494 feet (4,418 meters) above sea level.

The weather in this part of California is affected by elevation and the distance from the Pacific Ocean. Summer temperatures in the

This Mono woman poses with baskets made using traditional methods. In Mono culture, men and women played very specific roles. While women mainly prepared food and made crafts, men hunted and fished.

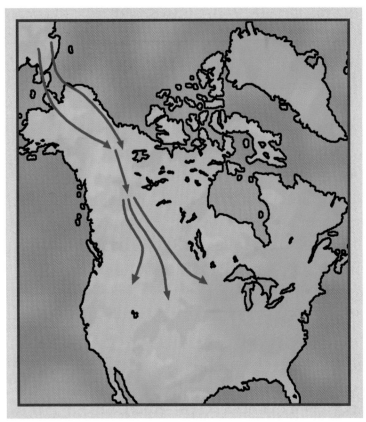

far south average higher than 100°F (38°C). In the Sierra Nevada highlands, the temperature rarely rises above 80°F (27°C). The average winter temperature in January ranges from below 10°F (-12°C) in the mountainous north to about 24°F (-4°C) in the far south. Each year the Western Mono's territories receive as much as 40 inches (102 centimeters) of water in the form of rain and snow. By contrast, the southern border of the Eastern Mono's territory is lucky to get 4 inches (10 cm).

Wherever they lived, the Mono depended on gathering wild plants, hunting, and fishing for everything that they ate. The men did most of the hunting, and the women and children gathered plants. Beyond this, the patterns of their way of life varied according to where they lived. The groups that made their homes on the western slopes of the Sierra Nevada had more water, plants, and animals than their eastern neighbors.

14   This map illustrates the routes taken by many of the Mono ancestors. By crossing a land bridge, early people migrated into North America following food sources.

Although much of the Native Americans' environment looked empty, it was actually filled with things that could be eaten. Because of droughts and other shortages, their willingness to eat almost anything was essential to their survival.

Throughout the region there were bighorn sheep, deer, bears, pronghorn antelope, and many other creatures. The streams and high lakes were the homes of dozens of kinds of fish. The land of the Mono also had an abundance of edible smaller creatures, including rabbits, gophers, insects, lizards, snakes, rats, mice, and birds. The Mono's territory also included hundreds of appetizing plants, including nuts, seeds, and edible roots, such as wild onions.

Villages and Camps

The Mono lived in villages and camps, at elevations that ranged from 500 to 10,000 feet (152 to 3,048 m). They relocated their settlements seasonally to take advantage of wild foods available during different months. Some communities moved more than others. The people who lived in the drier eastern highlands had to move the most. During the summers, many groups migrated into the cooler higher regions. During the winters, these communities often found shelter in the warmer valleys. Some Mono groups discovered that the land halfway between the peaks and the lower valleys had the most food resources. These types of areas are known as transitional life zones. In these places, the climate has less dramatic seasonal swings.

Because the weather does not change as drastically, many of the larger animals remain in these areas.

Some experts estimate that the average Mono community moved its residences over a trail that extended for about 40 miles (64 km). The need to frequently move made it difficult for the Mono to accumulate a lot of property. Everything had to be carried on their backs to the next village site.

The fact that natural resources were spread out over a large area limited the size of Mono villages. A community that lived in a place with abundant food rarely had more than fifty people. Some

16   Mount Whitney, located in the Mono territory, is one of the highest mountains in North America. It is measured at 14,494 feet (4,418 m) above sea level.

settlements had only one family. These smaller villages, or camps, might have had just five to twelve residents. When food was abundant, communities of all sizes would temporarily come together. These were happy times for the Native Americans. There were feasts, special ceremonies, and many games. These periods also allowed the Mono to meet with their distant relatives and friends. After the hunts and harvests, the larger group would divide into smaller communities, which would head out separately.

The Mono built houses that had round or oval floor plans. The upper part of the structures often looked like a dome. Some homes were cone shaped and looked a little like the hide-covered tepees used by the Native Americans who lived on the plains. Most of the houses were built on the level surface of the ground, although some were built inside shallow pits. The structures were 6 to 20 feet (1.8 to 6.1 m) in diameter. In order to create walls, wooden

All the Mono food resources came from the surrounding environment. Animals such as pronghorn antelope could be used in many aspects of Mono life.

poles were used with rocks, bark slabs, reeds, reed mats, grass, branches, or similar clusters of brush. In the center of each home, there was a fire pit that was lined with rocks. A hole in the roof allowed smoke to escape and light to enter the house. The entranceway was created by a short opening in the side wall that could be covered by a mat.

Most Mono villages had sweat houses. These buildings were similar to regular houses, except that they were sunk about 4 feet (1.2 m) into the ground. A large fire in the center of the sweat house filled the structure with smoke and intense heat. A trip to the sweat house was almost always followed by a swim in a nearby lake or stream. The Mono men used these buildings for recreation, for religious purposes, and as part of healing ceremonies. Hunters also spent time in the sweat houses before they went on an expedition. A special fire was created using sage as a fuel. The smoke made everyone smell like the wild plant. When the hunters went out the next day, the deer would not be able to smell them. The men and boys treated the sweat houses as a kind of club. In some Mono communities, they practically lived in the structures.

Cooking

Most Mono families ate two meals a day. The first was served early in the morning, shortly after dawn. The second meal took place in the afternoon. The women prepared most of the Mono dishes. They used many different cooking methods. Some of the foods that the Native Americans liked, such as wild berries, could be eaten raw. Other dishes required elaborate preparation. Many

In Mono culture, women were in charge of preparing meals. These Mono women, photographed in 1904, are processing acorn meal.

plants, such as acorns, had to be soaked in water for many hours in order to remove natural poisons.

One of the most common food preparation techniques was the grinding of plants, roots, and nuts into flour or powder using stone tools. The grinding implements included slab-like metates, which were used with small stones, called manos, to grind the food. The Mono also used something like a mortar and pestle to grind food. The mortar is a rock with circular holes and the pestle is a cylindrical stone that is used to pound food in the mortar. These tools could also be used to soften tough meat. Sometimes, smaller animals, insects, and fish

Sage was an important plant in the Mono culture. This strong plant flourishes in the sometimes harsh environment of the American West. Sage was burned ceremoniously in the Mono sweat houses.

were ground into powder, which was then added to stews and similar dishes as a flavoring. They also provided the Mono with extra vitamins and minerals.

The Mono had amazing cooking baskets. In order to cook a meal in one of these containers, the cook heated some small stones. Then she picked up the rocks with sticks and dropped them into the baskets, which were already filled with water and the other raw ingredients. The cook had to keep stirring the mixture, or one of the stones would settle to the bottom and burn a hole in the basket. By replacing the stones with other hot rocks, a Mono cook could even boil water.

Most of the Mono groups also cooked using ceramic bowls and jars. The pottery made it easy for the cooks to prepare foods like stews and acorn porridge.

Some Mono cooks used earth ovens to roast food. They would dig a deep pit in the ground and build a hot fire that would burn for several hours. The cooks took pieces of meat or vegetables and wrapped them up in leaves. They removed the fuel from the hole and replaced it with the food bundles. The pit was then covered with earth. After a few hours, the cooks would dig out the packets, which were now ready to be served.

The Mono sometimes preserved meat or fish for later use by smoking it. The flesh was cut into thin strips and placed on a wooden rack that stood above a small fire. Sometimes, tree branches were used instead of a rack. After a few hours, the fish or meat was ready to be stored for later use.

Every Mono cook tried to use whatever she could to get the most out of the plant or animal that she was preparing. The bones of larger animals were broken up to get the bone marrow. The skins of smaller animals, such as birds and lizards, were saved to make bags and clothing. Nothing was wasted.

22   This photo shows a typical cooking area in a Mono village. Much of the food the Mono ate was prepared in areas like these. Brush has been piled around the cooking space to control the wind.

Clothing and Body Decoration

The Mono's frequent relocations prevented them from developing elaborate types of clothing. Some of the things men and women wore were leather belts, caps, moccasins, shirts, and leggings. Some men had small pieces of deerskin suspended from their belts like loincloths. The Mono women usually wore skirts or aprons. Some had long dresses with sleeves. Small children did not wear clothing during the warm summer months. During the winter, everyone wore capes and blankets made from skin or fur.

When hunters went out to kill deer, they sometimes wore stuffed deer heads and deerskins. They even painted their legs white to look more like their targets. These disguises made it possible for them to get close to the deer and have a better chance at shooting the animals before they could run away.

Both the men and women had facial tattoos. They also loved jewelry made from bones, feathers, and seashells gained from trade. Some adornments were sewn onto clothing. The Mono wore necklaces and bracelets. Men and women pierced their ears and noses in order to use other ornaments. Facial paint and elaborate headdresses were used during special rituals.

Although water was often scarce, the Mono people emphasized cleanliness. Whenever they had the opportunity, they swam or bathed in streams and lakes.

24   Taken in the early 1900s, this photo of several children shows how the Mono wore both native and non-native clothing.

Arts and Crafts

The Mono were outstanding craftspeople. They used natural resources to produce hundreds of practical items for everyday use. These objects often incorporated beautiful designs.

The men transformed stones into many different kinds of tools. Items that required sharp edges were made by chipping. Pieces of obsidian, flint, basalt, and similar rocks were struck using other stones or bone hammers. The items they created included drills, spearheads, arrowheads, knives, and scrapers. Some stone tools were made by grinding the surfaces of harder pieces of rock together. These types of tools were made using granite, basalt, and sandstone. Some heavy stone tools, like metates and mortars, were left in place when the community moved.

The Mono women made baskets in many different shapes. Some were used as jars, fans, bottles, dishes, bowls, trays, caps, cradles, and boxes. In order to make different patterns, the women wove certain kinds of grasses, rushes, and tree shoots together into a single basket. By changing the materials, the Native Americans produced hundreds of geometric designs. The cooking baskets were woven so tightly that they could hold liquids. When it could be obtained, pitch, or the sap from pine trees, was used to line baskets to make them watertight.

Most Mono groups made pottery. Clay was dug out of streambeds and hillsides, and was then combined with sand and water. The wet mixture was formed into long snakelike pieces. These clay snakes were slowly coiled together to form pots and jars. Small round stones and wooden paddles were used to smooth the vessels' sides. The pots and jars had to be carefully dried in the sun before they could be stacked in a pit with brush and wood. The brush was ignited and the fire was allowed to burn for many hours. Once the pots and jars had completely cooled, they were ready to be used.

The Mono relied on many plants for crafts. Rushes and grasses were pounded into a cloth that could be used for blankets and skirts. Pieces of wood were transformed into digging sticks, musical instruments, clubs, throwing sticks (used in hunting), arrow shafts, spears, bowls, cups, ladles, stirring sticks, house poles, and trays. Plant fibers could be used to make strong threads or cords. The strands could even be woven together to fashion nets, bags, belts, and similar items. Bundles of reeds were combined to make rafts and crude canoes.

The animal world offered other important raw materials. Skins, furs, muscles, and sinews became cords, capes, skirts, loincloths, bags, ropes, belts, and blankets. Bones were transformed into flutes, combs, awls, beads, needles, hairpins, saws, and hammers. The Mono also incorporated bird feathers into arrows, headdresses, and ceremonial skirts. The tendons, or sinews, stripped from the legs of dead deer were combined with wood to make powerful bows.

Trade

The Mono traded with their western neighbors for many of the items they used. The Eastern Mono's territory was particularly rich in obsidian, a kind of volcanic glass used to make stone tools. Other items that were exchanged included rock salt, paint, baskets, and rabbit-skin

Baskets were widely used in Mono culture. They were also used in trade to gain items from other cultures.

blankets. The Eastern Mono also had abundant insects that were considered delicacies. The Western Mono, or Monache, traded with the eastern groups for rabbit skins, obsidian, and pine nuts. The eastern groups were largely interested in acorns. They also brought in soapstone, reeds for basket making, skins, arrows, baskets, seashell jewelry, and wild fruits. The Monache also worked as the middle men for their western neighbors, including the Yokut and the Miwok. It was unusual for the Mono to trade with groups that lived to the south, north, or east.

The Mono made a wide variety of beautiful yet practical baskets.

29

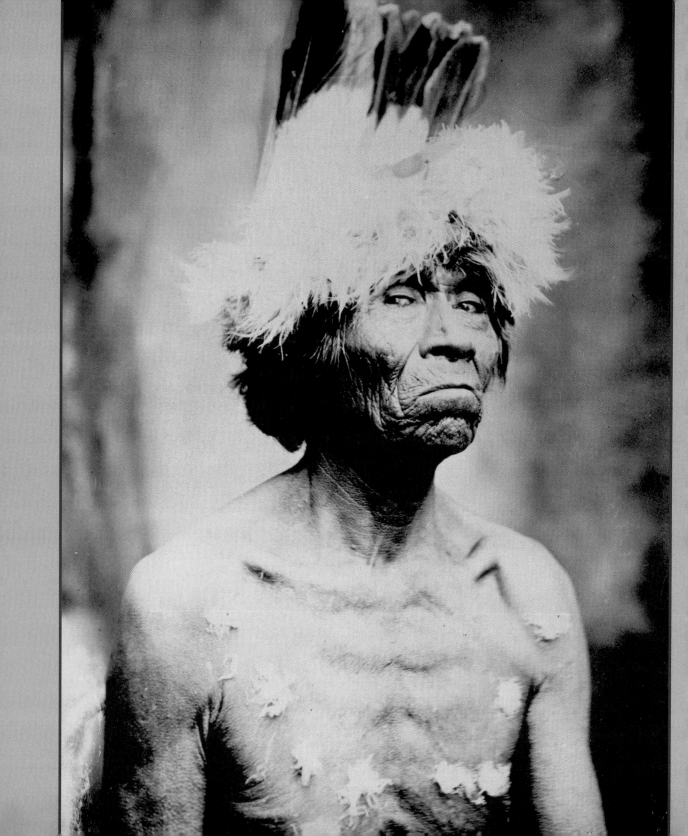

Three

Other Aspects of Mono Life

The Mono Nation used many different groups to create smaller social units. Membership in a particular group was based on where a person lived, who his or her parents were, and his or her wealth, sex, and age.

The smallest group was the family. The oldest man usually had the final word on decisions and work assignments. Some men, including village leaders, married several women. Marriages were often arranged by parents. Most villagers married members of other Mono settlements. The Western Mono spent a great deal of time interacting with their Yokut and Miwok neighbors. Not too surprisingly, they often married members of these groups.

Most Mono belonged to a particular clan. These people believed their families had a single animal ancestor, such as an eagle, mountain lion, or coyote. When people were born, they joined their father's clan. Among some Mono communities, several clans living together in a single village were divided into two parts. These social divisions helped to keep track of who was assigned to what work and other kinds of relations within society.

The largest social unit was the village. Although the Mono recognized some ties with other people who spoke similar languages, the early Mono people did not think of themselves in terms of tribes, nations, or other kinds of regional groups.

This Mono warrior was 105 years old when this photograph was taken in 1905. Many war medals are carved into his chest.

Every Mono village had its own political leader or chief. These men were usually members of the eagle clan. They received special gifts from their followers. However, they gave these objects back to the community during times of crisis or religious celebration. Some chiefs were selected because their fathers had been leaders. In many communities, a new chief was elected on the basis of his abilities. In some villages, the chiefs had helpers. These people were often members of his family or village elders. They assisted the chiefs by serving as messengers and advisers. Because the communities kept moving, it was difficult for a person to accumulate wealth. The Mono basically thought of everyone in their society as equals.

Most Mono settlements also had people who worked as part-time religious leaders and doctors. These people kept objects and performed rituals that had special powers. These holy men had extraordinary dreams in which they were given supernatural capabilities by spirits or ancestors. The doctors were respected by all the members of their societies. Many of the common people feared them because they sometimes used their powers to hurt their enemies.

Government

The Mono did not have any overarching government system. In most of the Mono territory, each village claimed the areas where its people hunted, fished, and gathered. A person from outside the community who wanted to enter this area had to get permission from the chief, or he would be treated as a thief. The chiefs usually settled any fights that broke out between members of the same village. It is important to understand that the village leaders did not have absolute power. They usually led by example and could not do much if someone decided to disobey them.

Warfare

The Mono people rarely turned to warfare as a way of solving their problems. They would defend themselves when they were attacked or if they felt that they had to protect their community resources. Wars sometimes broke out when one community accused another of having religious leaders who had used supernatural forces to hurt them. Of all the people who lived close to the Mono, only the Washo were generally thought of as unfriendly and dangerous.

Family feuds within villages sometimes ended in violence. These struggles were usually short, and few people were hurt or killed. It was extremely unusual for an entire community to be eliminated or for a settlement to be destroyed. The village chiefs worked hard to prevent this kind of violence from getting out of hand.

When Mono warriors went out to battle, the village chief usually led the men. The fighters relied on spears and bows and arrows as weapons. The lack of armor, shields, and other protective equipment reflects the Mono's limited interest in warfare.

34   This photo, taken in 1872, shows three Paiute men wearing elaborate clothing and feather war bonnets. This photo was probably staged in order to support the white man's image of what Native Americans wore when hunting or fighting in war.

Hunting and Fishing

The Mono men were extremely good hunters and fishers. They enjoyed going on hunting expeditions with their dogs. They hunted and ate nearly all of the animals that they found. The most common weapon they used was the bow and arrow. The Mono also used spears, snares, and L-shaped throwing sticks. The hunters would sometimes use nets that were several hundred feet long. They would stretch the snare across the front of a ravine, then drive small animals, like rabbits, into the trap. When they went out to hunt deer, the men often wore deerskins and antler headdresses as disguises. Occasionally, other animals such as antelopes were driven into narrow canyons where they became easy targets for Mono archers. The hunters also created hiding places near trails using rocks or brush. When large animals came near, they would kill them with a well-placed arrow.

The Mono who lived near lakes, rivers, and streams developed many techniques for fishing. Some groups used large nets. Other people specialized in the use of spears or hunted fish with arrows. Many of the Mono built small dams in shallow waters to force fish into brush traps or baskets.

Religion

The Mono Nation had its own special ideas about gods and the supernatural world. These beliefs helped the Native Americans make sense of the world that surrounded them. They also provided them with important ideals so that they could live as good people. Most of the Mono's religious ceremonies were held in order to keep the people's lives and world in balance.

Three of the most important ceremonies were the bear dance, the rattlesnake dance, and the annual mourning ceremony. Each of these rituals helped to insure the well-being of the community. Many of the religious holidays were tied to the annual cycle of food harvests. During these events, the Mono offered thanks for the community's survival or attempted to get the help of supernatural forces.

When large numbers gathered for holidays, the Mono also liked to gamble using sticks or bones for markers. Some individuals participated in or bet on competitive sports like running.

When the Mono people celebrated, they often sang and

36 The rattlesnake was a feared and respected figure in the Mono culture. Many animals were incorporated into Mono religious beliefs.

danced. The human voice provided much of the music. Native instruments included a wide variety of rattles, clapping sticks, whistles, and flutes. The musicians also used a piece of bone or wood tied to the end of a stone to make a whirling sound. They did not have drums. During these rituals, religious leaders often wore special body paint, clothing, and feathered headdresses.

Important rituals also marked the various stages of a person's life. There were rites for birth, adulthood, and death. The Mono had elaborate funerals. The bodies were carefully buried a short time after the person died. The person's property was burned over his or her grave. A second funeral was held about one year later. Special dances and songs were performed to help the spirit of a dead person on the journey into the afterlife. The Mono believed that he or she would reach the land of the dead within two days after death.

The Mono sometimes marked the faces of rocks with symbols. These designs were scratched onto the surface of large stones. These images are called petroglyphs. Many other native nations painted similar images on rocks. These types of decorations, known as pictographs, were not made by the Mono. We do not understand why the Mono made rock art and choose not to use paint. Many people believe that the symbols were created during religious ceremonies. Because places with rock art are sacred to many modern Native Americans, it is essential that everyone show respect when they view them.

Four

Dealing with the Newcomers

For centuries after the European discovery of America, the Mono people continued their traditional way of life. In 1540, the first Europeans reached southern California. More than 200 years would pass before the first Spanish colony was created at San Diego. During this period, the European explorers never reached the lands of the Mono, who were hidden by the immense geographic barriers of the Sierra Nevada and the Mojave Desert. These natural defenses were stronger than anything that the Mono could build.

Despite the fact that explorers did not come into direct contact with the Mono, their presence in California still influenced the Native Americans who lived in the interior. Europeans introduced a wide variety of horrible diseases into the Americas.

These illnesses spread into the interior of the continents when coastal people went on trading expeditions, or sometimes they simply spread from one person to the next when they spoke to one another. Diseases also invaded central and eastern California with the migration of animals and insects, such as mosquitos.

While we do not have any written records for the Mono during this period, they probably had to cope with new diseases, such as measles and smallpox. The natives had never seen these sicknesses before. It is likely that the illnesses killed many people, just as they

The mission system would challenge the traditional way of life for many Native Americans. This painting, done in 1877 by artist Leon Trousset, illustrates the scene of the dedication of mission headquarters at Monterey, California, in 1771.

had in other regions of North America. The populations of some native nations were reduced by as much as 90 percent. That means that nine out of every ten Mono may have died of European diseases between 1520 and 1769.

The Mono Versus Spanish and Mexican California

Between 1769 and 1821, the Spanish empire created a series of twenty-one missions and four military bases (presidios) on the coast of California. Although the priests developed plans to create more missions in the interior, shortages of resources and changes in government policies prevented them from achieving their goals. The Mono remained outside of the area under Spanish control.

During this period, there were a number of Spanish explorers who came close to the borders of the Mono homeland. Pedro Fages, Francisco Garcés, and Gabriel Moraga passed through areas that were less than 100 miles (161 km) from the closest Mono village. The Native Americans living beyond the Sierra Nevada probably heard stories about the strangers and their horses and guns.

Despite the fact that the Mono did not have direct contact with the invaders, all of California's Native Americans were gradually subjected to a series of major changes. These transformations were the indirect consequences of the presence of the distant Spanish colony. Many of these repercussions threatened Mono customs and traditions. Parts of the old trading network collapsed as the coastal peoples to the west joined the Europeans in the mission system. Fierce struggles broke out as Native Americans attempted to gain a foothold in the new European trade system. European animals and plants spread from the coast into the interior without the aid of humans, often doing terrible damage to the environment.

The Europeans brought many kinds of new plants, insects, and animals to California. Many of these, such as weeds and rats, were brought by accident in the cargos of ships. Numerous new arrivals thrived in California. Because they had developed in other parts of the world, some of these biological invaders had no natural enemies. In some places, escaped cattle, horses, donkeys, and sheep simply ate up all of the Native Americans' traditional plant food. In other regions, it became clear that many of the native grasses and animals could not compete against the more aggressive newcomers. Within a few decades, the new plants and animals expanded their range eastward.

Although the invaders introduced many horrors, their arrival also brought opportunities. Native Americans who did not like the missions escaped into the interior and eventually to Mono territory. They brought many new ideas that the Mono used to improve their hunting and gathering. Some groups experimented with growing plants such as tobacco. As sheep, horses, cattle, and mules found their way into the interior, the Native Americans learned to hunt them as a new source of food. Soon, they were also riding horses. Native Americans from all over the western United States developed a desire for the invaders' practical steel tools, firearms, and decorative clothing.

By 1835, horses and mules had become an important feature of daily life among the Native Americans who lived in the Central Valley of California, to the west of the Western Mono. Horses made it easier to hunt and to fight. Both horses and mules made it possible for communities to move large amounts of baggage from village site to site. It is unclear how much of the horse culture crossed the Sierra Nevada. At the very least, the Mono must have become aware of the desirability of gaining access to these four-legged wonders.

42   This painting, done by Frederic Remington, depicts Jedediah Smith's expedition across the harsh desert environment to reach Spanish settlements at San Diego. In 1827, Smith would visit lands very close to the Mono territory.

In 1827, the American mountain man Jedediah Smith followed a trail that led him into the region just north of the Eastern Mono. Six years later, Joseph R. Walker crossed over part of the Mono homeland. In 1834, he led a party of pioneers down through the heart of the Owens Valley. These mountain men were mostly interested in the skins of beavers and similar animals. They passed through the region quickly and had little contact with the native peoples. However, their arrival marked the beginning of a new era. Invaders from the United States, Great Britain, and Mexico increasingly moved through the eastern parts of California seeking trade and new lands to settle. After 1835, commerce involving European goods dramatically increased. Steel knives, wool blankets, guns, and horses were more readily available, even for remote people like the Mono.

The Mono and the Americans

Between 1845 and 1847, the republics of Mexico and the United States fought over the future of the western part of North America. The Mono undoubtedly noted the party of American explorers made up of Joseph Walker, Richard Owens, Ed Kern, Kit Carson, and John C. Frémont, when it crossed through their country in 1845. The maps that these men made would guide later parties of explorers. However, to the Mono, like most Native Americans, the movement of the confused travelers seemed unimportant.

When the war ended, the territory of California was transferred from Mexico to the United States. The discovery of gold in the Sierra

Nevada brought a previously unknown number of newcomers to the region. Within a few years, the miners began to move to the south and east in search of new mineral discoveries. In 1852, gold was discovered in the Mono Basin. The Mono's territory was soon filled with invaders who considered the Native Americans to be wild creatures that should either be killed or forced to move away.

As the mining frontier expanded, the Mono found themselves with few options. The invaders often rounded up and simply murdered Native Americans. Whole communities of Mono, which had existed for thousands of years, were destroyed. In mining towns such as Aurora, Nevada, and Bodie and Cerro Gordo, California, the native people were forced to live as beggars or were captured and turned into slaves. The miners' towns and industries polluted the land and water. Terrible damage was done to the delicate mountain and desert

Kit Carson would become one of the great heroes of the Old West. Born in 1809, Carson made a reputation for himself as a fearless guide and soldier. Much of his later career would be dedicated to improving relations between natives and Americans.

environments. Hundreds of thousands of precious trees were cut down to be used as fuel. The Mono who lived close to the miners also caught horrible new diseases that left them sick or dead.

Most California government officials were pleased about what was happening. In 1850, Governor Peter Burnett expressed the hope that every native person should die. Although not all the invaders agreed with such racist ideas, few of them were willing or powerful enough to stop the terrible destruction.

By 1859, some Paiute in the Owens Valley were ready to fight back. Their horses allowed them to raid as far as the San Fernando

Once a wild and untouched land, the territory of the Mono would be ravaged by the California gold rush. This photo shows a mining town scarring the land in 1859.

Valley, near Los Angeles. The first army column to enter the valley was led by Captain John Davidson. He promised the peaceful people that they would be left alone, as long as they let white people pass in peace. However, the newcomers soon broke their word.

Things went from bad to worse during the terrible winter of 1861 to 1862. Mono people were starving, and they killed and ate the horses, cattle, and sheep of the invaders, which was the only available food. Besides, these creatures were eating many of the plants that the Mono depended on. The livestock owners demanded that the army punish the Mono. They wanted the peaceful Mono to be treated like savage thieves.

Fighting broke out even before the army had arrived in the Mono territory. At first, it was bows and arrows against the settlers' rifles and six-shooters. Several skirmishes were fought, followed by a number of attempts by leaders to make peace. The Native Americans found merchants in Aurora who would sell them guns and ammunition. These same men refused to sell anything to the Owens Valley ranchers and miners. They told their fellow white men that they were on the Mono's side. When word of the brewing trouble reached the army at Fort Tejon, a column of troops was sent to help the settlers. The Mono used their new guns to win several small victories. The army expedition had to retreat when it ran out of supplies.

The Mono continued to resist. In July 1862, the army decided to create a supply base in the Owens Valley. The outpost was called Camp Independence. The Mono now had to face the army as well as roving bands of settlers. Their struggle climaxed in a battle fought

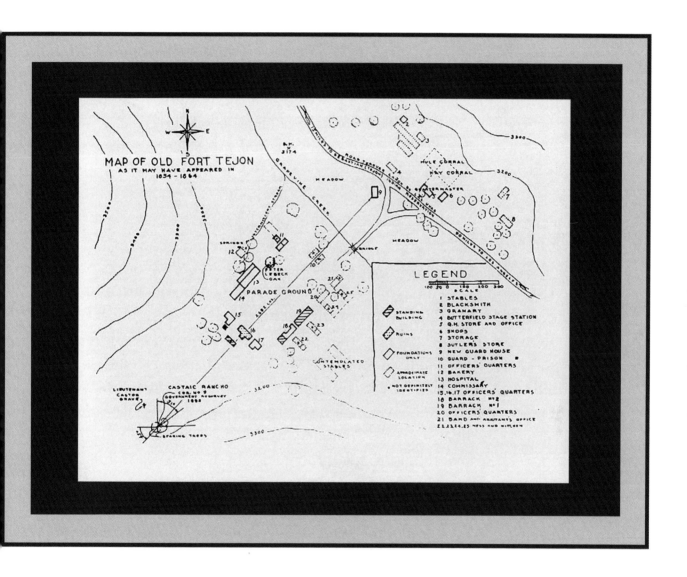

The above map shows the layout of Fort Tejon. The United States military used forts like this to protect settlers from the Native Americans. Many forts would eventually be turned into trading posts and play an important role in Native American-United States relations.

at Bishop. The fifty well-armed settlers reported that they had defeated about 500 Native Americans. The army also continued its attacks. The troops made it a point to burn any stored food that they found. The Mono's guns, which had been the key to their success, had worn out. No one knew how to repair them. Their rusty barrels sometimes exploded. Other weapons began to misfire.

By the spring of 1863, it was clear that the Owens Valley war would end in a U.S. victory. Between May and July 1863, most of the Mono surrendered. Almost 1,000 Native Americans were marched as prisoners to the reservation at San Sebastian, near Fort Tejon. Mono leader Joaquin Jim was the only chief who refused to give up. He and his warriors continued to fight for another year and a half. Finally, in December 1864, the army cornered Jim's band. The troops killed him and most of his followers.

In 1869, a Shoshone holy man, Wodziwob, received a vision of a new future for Native Americans. He believed that special rituals could cause the white invaders to suddenly disappear. If they followed the right path, the native lands and original animals would return. Wodziwob's ideas inspired many Native Americans, including the Mono. The new religious movement reached its peak under the leadership of Wodziwob's son, Wovoka. Among the Mono and many other California followers, the faith did not include any form of armed resistance. Sadly, these new native visions were not fulfilled, although some parts of the religion continue to be practiced today.

By 1875, the miners were less of a threat to the surviving Mono than farmers, ranchers, and sheepherders. Some of the best gathering

Wovoka, photographed here in 1916, would lead a spiritual revolution for Native Americans. Wovoka's movement called for a peaceful resistance of the Americans. He imagined a world without the white man, where native people could return to their old ways.

places were taken over by farmers. Wheat, fruit trees, and vegetable patches replaced wild food sources. Meanwhile, tens of thousands of head of livestock ate most of the plants that had survived. The newcomers also set up barbed-wire fences. These barriers prevented wild animals from making traditional migrations. As a result, some types of creatures quickly disappeared from the Mono land.

Some of the Mono complained to government officials. They wanted to know why some Native Americans had reservations, but the Mono had no place to call their own. They were told that they should move to western Nevada to the Paiute Reservation that had

The rerouting of water systems by the city of Los Angeles would radically change the landscape of parts of the Mono world.

been created in 1874. However, most Mono did not feel that it would be right to move in with people that they did not know, to lands where they would be foreigners.

Despite its misfortunes, the nation used its creative energy to preserve many of its traditions. By 1900, some outsiders were also helping to save native peoples. They recognized that the Mono were being treated unfairly. In 1912, the Western Mono were given small reservations at North Fork, Big Sandy, and Cold Springs in California. That same year, a large area of land was granted to the Eastern Mono. It was called the Paiute Reservation of California. During the decades that followed, the Eastern Mono were granted smaller amounts of land at Bishop (1913), Fort Independence (1915), Big Pine (1922), and Lone Pine (1939). Gradually, jobs opened up for Mono in logging, shepherding, and ranching. By the middle of the twentieth century, most of the surviving groups had English or Hispanic family names. Still, the language and many other important Mono customs lived on.

While the first reservations were being created, another force was bringing changes that would have horrible consequences. All of the people who lived in the Owens Valley, both Native Americans and newcomers, suffered a great loss when the Los Angeles Department of Power and Water purchased their water rights. The department's efforts started in 1905. Eight years later, the project began to send the valley's water resources south to Los Angeles. The green color of the valley was replaced by brown grass and sagebrush. Most of the jobs that were available to Native Americans also disappeared. Owens Lake finally dried up completely in 1927. It has remained without water ever since.

Five

The Mono Today

The United States's program designed to eliminate the Native Americans as a community continued through the middle of the twentieth century. Gradually, the national government gave up on some of its worst policies. Native Americans worked hard for the recognition of their human rights. After World War I, pressure grew for fair treatment of Native Americans. In 1924, Native Americans were finally granted the status of U.S. citizens.

By 1930, most Mono men worked on highway construction crews and helped out at ranches. The native communities still hunted and gathered some of their food. The people made traditional houses, baskets, metates, and rabbit-skin blankets. Some traditional medicines were prepared. However, many of the old customs were disappearing.

As the century progressed, there were still terrible setbacks that would come to the Mono Nation. In 1932, the government eliminated the tribe's ownership of its largest single property, the Paiute Reservation. In 1958, the Western Mono reservations at Big Sandy, Cold Springs, and North Fork were also eliminated. Many of the Native Americans fought these government actions. They knew that the elimination of the reservations would bring an end to economic

Water briefly collects in Owens Dry Lake after a summer storm. Once a jewel of the Mono territory, the lake has dried up from the transferring of water rights to the city of Los Angeles.

The Mono people have survived centuries of hardships imposed by Americans.

opportunities and many special programs in education and health care that other Native Americans received. Many tribal leaders also realized that the elimination of reservations would help to end their sense of identity.

Since 1958, the government stopped its programs designed to eliminate reservations. The Western Mono communities at Big Sandy and North Fork were reinstated as federal reservations in 1983. The Eastern Mono of the Bridgeport Indian Colony were granted government recognition in 1974. Other groups of Mono people, including the Mono Lake Indian Community and the Dunlap Band of Mono Indians, are still seeking government recognition. No one is sure how many Mono people live off the reservation. The overall Mono population has steadily grown since 1970. By 2000, its numbers exceeded 3,000.

The people of the Mono Nation are working hard to create jobs and reclaim their heritage. Money-making endeavors, like the Paiute Palace Casino, in Bishop, California, represent only one small part of the new Mono world. Of even greater importance has been the creation of heritage institutions, such as the Owens Valley Paiute-Shoshone Cultural Center. The Mono continue the struggle to save their traditional sacred places, such as Coso Hot Springs. Tribal leaders are also fighting hard to preserve and restore the delicate desert environment that surrounds them.

So much of the old world of early California has vanished. Few people experienced more changes to their homeland than the Mono.

Still, their will to survive as a people has never ended. Some extraordinary force has made it possible for them to continue with courage. That mysterious force can still be seen in the eyes of the Mono today. The people's determination and spirit promise to carry them into a brighter future. By continuing their ancient customs and making their own unique contributions to the modern world, the Mono's existence will benefit all the people of the United States.

Coso Hot Springs in Inyo County, California, was enjoyed by the Mono for the water's healing effects.

Timeline

13,000–40,000 years ago	The ancestors of the Shoshone nations arrive in North America from Asia.
6,000–8,000 years ago	Native peoples who are the ancestors of the Shoshone people settle in the area of what is now Nevada.
5,000–3,500 years ago	Shoshone-speaking people move to the south and west into what is today eastern California. Among these people are the ancestors of the Mono.
AD 1540–1769	Europeans explore areas of coastal California. They introduce diseases that are likely to have significantly reduced the size of the Mono population.
1769–1835	The Spanish and Mexican governments establish a chain of missions, towns, and military bases along the California coast.
1835–1846	Increasing numbers of American fur trappers and merchants from New Mexico trade with Native Americans living in the interior, including the Mono people.

1846–1848	The United States conquers California. The Mono Nation now lives in a region claimed by the United States.
1849	The gold rush begins in the Sierra Nevada.
1859–1863	Some Owens Valley Paiutes (Eastern Mono) attempt to fight back against invaders. They are defeated. More than 900 are forced into exile at Fort Tejon.
1912–present	Various Mono groups are recognized as native nations by the government. Some are granted lands that become reservations.
1913	Los Angeles begins to pump water out of the Owens Valley.
1924	All Native Americans are made U.S. citizens.
1954	Many of the Mono reservations are disbanded by the United States government.
1983	The Western Mono reservations of Big Sandy Rancería and North Fork Rancería are restored.

Glossary

afterlife (AF-ter-lyf) Existence after death.

clan (KLAN) A group united by a common characteristic.

metate (meh-TAH-tay) A slab-like piece of stone with a depression that is used to grind food with a mano, or small stone.

mission system (MI-shon SIS-tum) A system used to spread religious beliefs and goodwill to another country or region.

mortar (MOR-tur) A large stone with circular holes in which food is ground; used with a pestle.

pestle (PEH-suhl) A cylinder-shaped stone that is used with a mortar to grind food.

petroglyphs (PEH-troh-gliffs) Rock art that has designs created using scratching or carving.

pictographs (PIK-toh-graffs) Rock art that has designs created using paint.

rock art (ROK ART) A form of art that involves scratching, carving, or painting designs or pictures on large rock surfaces.

sinew (SIN-yoo) A tendon.

Resources

BOOKS

Bahr, Diana Meyers, and Viola Martinez. *California Paiute: Living in Two Worlds*. Norman, OK: University of Oklahoma Press, 2003.

Campbell, Paul D. *Survival Skills of Native Californians*. Salt Lake City: Gibbs Smith, 1999.

Malinowski, Sharon, ed. *Gale Encyclopedia of Native American Tribes*. Detroit: Gale Group, 1998.

Rawl, James J. *Indians of California: The Changing Image*. Norman, OK: University of Oklahoma Press, 1986.

Stanley, Terry. *Digger: The Tragic Fate of the California Indians from the Missions to the Gold Rush*. New York: Crown Publishing, 1997.

MUSEUMS

Eastern California Museum
155 North Grant Street
P.O. Box 206
Independence, CA 93526
(760) 878-0364
This museum offers exhibits that explore the region's complex history, including the presence of Native Americans.

Owens Valley Paiute-Shoshone Cultural Center
2301 West Line Street
Bishop, CA 93514
(760) 873-4478
This institution has exhibits and activities that are created and
maintained by Native Americans.

WEB SITES

Due to the changing nature of Internet links, the Rosen Publishing
Group, Inc., has developed an online list of Web sites related to
the subject of this book. This site is updated regularly. Please use
this link to access the list:

http://www.rosenlinks.com/lnac/mono

Index